EXPLORE ECOSYSTEMS

IN A POND

SARAH RIDLEY

WAYLAND

First published in Great Britain in 2022 by Wayland

Editor: Amy Pimperton
Designer: Lisa Peacock
Picture researchers: Diana Morris, Sarah Ridley

ISBN: 978 1 5263 2245 6 (hardback); 978 1 5263 2246 3 (paperback)

Printed and bound in China

Wayland, an imprint of
Hachette Children's Group
Part of Hodder & Stoughton
Carmelite House
50 Victoria Embankment
London EC4Y 0DZ
An Hachette UK Company
www.hachelle.co.uk
www.hachettechildrens.co.uk

Picture acknowledgements:
Alamy: DPWildlife Invertebrates 10.
Nature PL: Stephen Dalton 15b; Jan Hamrsky 11c; Ross Hoddinott/2020Vision 4;
David Kjaer 22; Remi Masson 20; Sinclair Stammers 9t; Kim Taylor 16, 26; Nick Upton 12.
Shutterstock: Albert Beukhof f cover bl, 27b; Coulanges 21t; davemhuntphotography 21b;
Deborde f cover br; Alexander Denisenko 1t, 6c; Dr Pixel 28; Dirk Ercken 23;
Martin Fowler 13t; Jamie Hall 27t, 33; kajasja 25b; Patrick Keirsebilck 29t;
Matteo Photos 18; Martin Mecnarowski 29b; Meunierd 24; Stas Moroz 25t; M600i 30t;
MVolodymyr 5t; Nkula 7; Rudolf Otrokov 9bl; Martin Pelanek 1b, 14; Pyty 30b;
Fabio Sacchi 3, 11r; Jordan Sharp 17; Simikov 9br; AndrewASkolnick 13b;
Slowmotiongli 15t; Rostislav Stafanek 6br; W de Vries 18b, 9t, 22-23c;
Clark Warren1991 19b; Wirestock Creators f cover t; Harry Wolverson 5b.

Every attempt has been made to clear copyright. Should there be any
inadvertent omission please apply to the publisher for rectification.

Always be careful near water! If you plan to visit a pond, take a trusted adult with you.

Ponds can be dangerous since they are often deeper than they look. Never go too close to a pond or river without adult supervision.

Contents

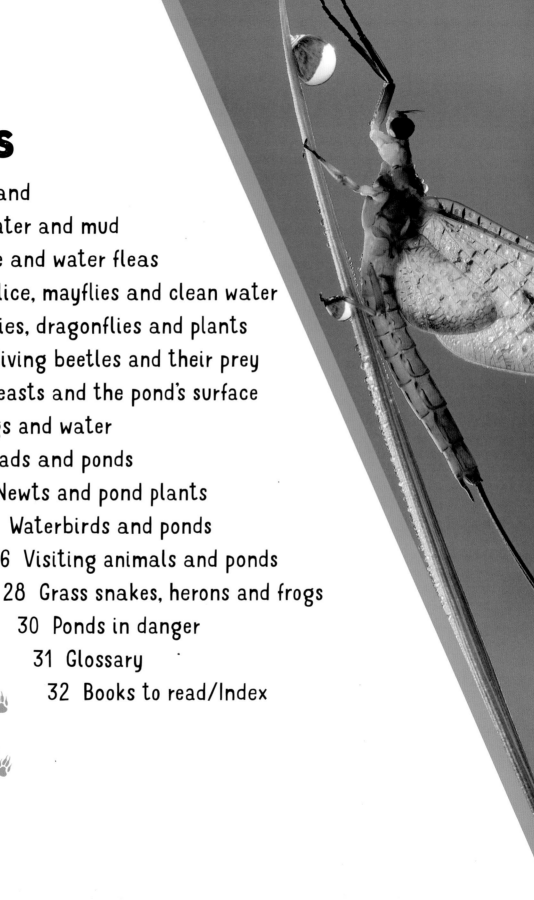

A pond ecosystem is all the living things and non-living things in a pond, and the different ways they are connected to each other.

Pond in a farm field

Ponds and the land

There are ponds in gardens, parks and wild areas all around the world.

A pond is an area of still, fresh water, usually smaller than a lake.
Some ponds form when water collects in a dip or hollow in the land.
Most ponds were dug by people to provide drinking water for animals
or to make special places in gardens, parks and wildlife areas.

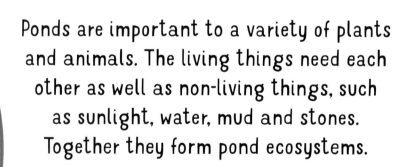

Ducks in a pond
in the rain

Water stays in a pond
because a pond's sides
and bottom are made from a
layer of clay, mud or stones.
While some ponds are filled
by an underground spring
or human-made water pipe,
others collect rainwater.

Horse drinking from a pond

Ponds are important to a variety of plants
and animals. The living things need each
other as well as non-living things, such
as sunlight, water, mud and stones.
Together they form pond ecosystems.

Ponds need fresh water, mud
and stones to stay as ponds.

Water lilies, water and mud

Water lilies are perfectly adapted to their watery habitat.
Their roots grow through mud and stones at the bottom of a pond
to hold the plant in place. Long stems grow up towards the light.

Water lilies

Water lily stems

The stems hold the leaves and flowers above the
pond's surface to attract insect pollinators.

The large leaves are called lily pads. They float on the water, making food for the plant by soaking up sunlight and carbon dioxide, as well as nutrients from pond water. This is called photosynthesis.

Frog on a lily pad

Lily pads provide shade, shelter and food to pond animals. However, some predators, including frogs, use them as a hunting ground, so pond animals need to watch out!

Water lily roots need pond mud and stones, while lily pads need water to float on the surface.

Plants, algae and water fleas

Pond plants and algae are at the bottom of every pond food chain. Like water lilies, they make their own food through the process of photosynthesis (see page 7).

Hornwort is a very important pond plant as it releases oxygen into pond water during photosynthesis. Many pond animals, including newts, use this oxygen to stay alive.

Smooth newt

Hornwort

Algae also release oxygen into pond water through photosynthesis. Algae are eaten by tiny animals called water fleas.

A water flea uses its legs to bring water into its mouth. Here it filters algae, bacteria and other tiny living things out of the water and eats them. Water fleas keep ponds healthy by eating algae. If too much grows, algae can cover the pond's surface, blocking out sunlight and killing pond life.

Water flea

Algae-covered pond

Algae with oxygen bubbles

Pond plants and algae release oxygen into pond water. All animals need oxygen to stay alive.

Water hoglouse

Water hoglice, mayflies and clean water

When plants die, they sink to the bottom of ponds and start to rot.
Minibeasts, including mayfly larvae and water hoglice, eat them.
This helps to clean up the water and keeps the pond ecosystem healthy.

Water hoglice are also called water slaters. They spend their
lives crawling about underwater, rather than swimming.

Mayfly larvae are the young of mayflies. The larvae eat algae as well as dead plants, helping to recycle left-over nutrients into their growing bodies.

Mayfly larva

Adult mayfly

Adult mayflies live for only a few days. They mate and the females lay their eggs in ponds and rivers to start the life cycle again. Young and adult mayflies are eaten by a lots of different pond creatures.

Pond minibeasts, such as hoglice, eat dead plants, which helps to keep pond water clean.

Damselflies, dragonflies and plants

When a mayfly takes to the air, it has to watch out for predators!

Damselflies and dragonflies hunt other flying insects such as mosquitoes, flies and moths. They snatch prey out of the air, but need to rest on pond plants to eat.

Mayfly

Damselfly

Female dragonfly laying eggs

Damselflies and dragonflies need pond plants throughout their lives. This dragonfly is laying her eggs among pond plants. Other species push their eggs into plant stems.

Once the larvae, or nymphs, hatch, they hide among underwater plants at the bottom of the pond. If a tadpole or insect larva comes close, the nymph grabs its prey!

Adult dragonfly

When it's time to change into an adult, a nymph crawls up a plant stem at the edge of the pond, sheds its skin and starts its life as an adult insect.

Dragonflies and damselflies need pond plants in different ways throughout their life cycle.

Dragonfly nymph skin

13

Great diving beetle

Great diving beetles and their prey

Great diving beetles visit the pond's surface for air. They collect an air bubble, store it under their wings and use it to breathe underwater for up to 30 minutes.

When a great diving beetle wants to move to a different pond, it uses its wings to take off and fly.

Adult diving beetles and their larvae hunt a wide variety of prey including tadpoles, insect larvae, newts and pond snails. The larvae have large jaws that they sink into their prey before sucking out the prey's insides.

Great diving beetle eating a bloodworm

Great diving beetle larva and tadpole

Adult diving beetles use their jaws to tear prey apart. Long, hairy back legs act like oars to pull their body through water. They are speedy pond predators, but can become prey for newts or waterbirds.

Healthy pond ecosystems need predators that eat other animals.

Minibeasts and the pond's surface

When this fly fell into a pond it created ripples. These attracted the attention of an insect called a pond skater. It raced across the pond's surface to stab the fly with its sharp mouth and suck up the fly's juices.

Pond skater with fly

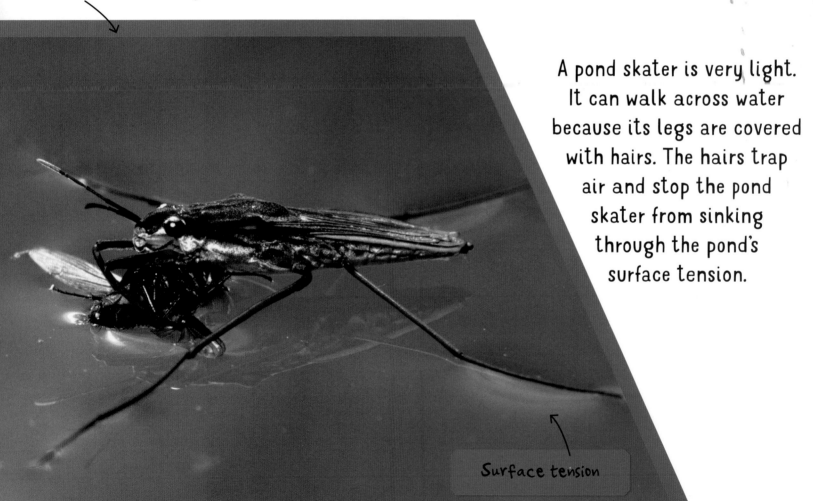

A pond skater is very light. It can walk across water because its legs are covered with hairs. The hairs trap air and stop the pond skater from sinking through the pond's surface tension.

Surface tension

The non-living surface of a pond provides a hunting ground for pond skaters, raft spiders and other pond animals.

Surface tension

Raft spider

A raft spider is much bigger than a pond skater, but walks across water in the same way. It lurks at the edge of a pond with its front legs resting on the water's surface to pick up the movement of prey. Its prey includes insects, as well as tadpoles and small fish.

Common frogs mating

Frogspawn

Frogs and water

Frogs gather in ponds during the early months of the year.
It's time to find a mate and lay eggs.

When the male frog holds the female, it makes her release eggs. She
can lay up to 5,000 eggs in one go. Each egg is surrounded by jelly.
When the tadpoles hatch a few weeks later, they eat the jelly and
then move on to eating algae, plants and pond insects.

Tadpole

Froglet

Over the next two or three months, the tadpoles grow and change. Each tadpole grows lungs to replace its gills, back legs then front legs. Its tail shrinks until it becomes a froglet. Now it can leave the water.

Froglets and frogs spend the summer in and around ponds where there are plenty of minibeasts to hunt and they can keep their skin damp. Some frogs hibernate at the bottom of ponds over the winter.

Ponds provide frogs with the perfect watery place to live at different stages in their life cycle.

Common toad among strings of eggs

Toads and ponds

Toads also need ponds to breed.

Like frogs, they often return to the pond where they hatched. This can bring many toads to the same pond each spring. As they mate, female toads lay strings of eggs among pond plants. In about ten days' time, tadpoles will hatch.

At first toad tadpoles eat algae and plants, but they swop these for insects as they grow. Like frog tadpoles, they grow back legs then front legs, until they become tiny toads about three months later. Toads and toad tadpoles taste bad to many predators, which helps them to survive life in a pond.

Toad tadpole

All adult amphibians, including toads and frogs, can live on land and in water. Toads spend most of their lives away from ponds. Over winter they shelter under stones or logs, or in burrows.

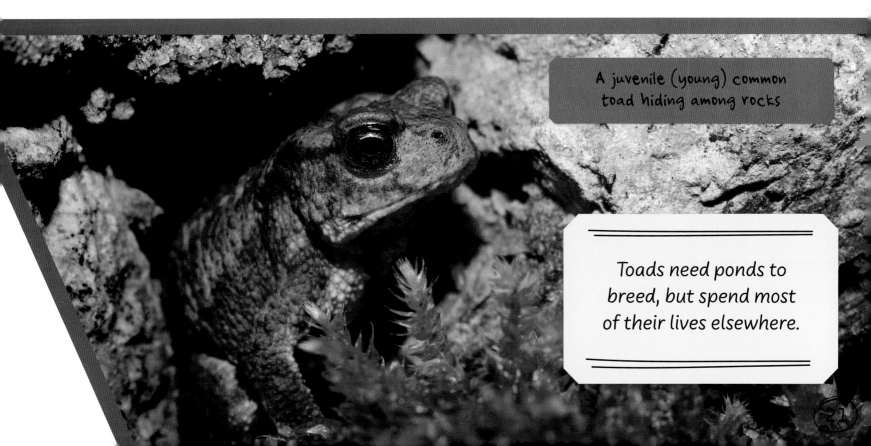

A juvenile (young) common toad hiding among rocks

Toads need ponds to breed, but spend most of their lives elsewhere.

Newts and pond plants

Like frogs and toads, newts travel to ponds in the spring.
This is where they mate and lay eggs.

A female newt spends hours laying up to 300 eggs. It takes so long because she wraps each egg in the leaf of a pond plant, to protect it from predators.

Male (top) and female (bottom) great crested newts

Newt eggs in folded leaves

Unlike frog and toad tadpoles, newt tadpoles grow front legs before back legs, and have frilly gills around their heads for breathing. It takes about three months for a tadpole to grow and change into a small adult newt.

Newt tadpole

Newts need pond water and pond plants to breed and hunt.

Adult newts spend the spring and summer in and around ponds. They hunt insects and other minibeasts on land and in water. Over winter they hibernate under stones or branches until spring.

Waterbirds and ponds

Most waterbirds live in river or lake habitats,
but some make large ponds their home.

This Canada goose used pond plants to build her nest beside a pond and
lined it with feathers. Her mate will defend her and the nest from predators.

Canada goose, nest and eggs

Mallards are ducks. Female ducks build nests in secret places near fresh water. When her ducklings hatch, the mother leads them to water. She shows her ducklings which plants and insects are good to eat.

Ducks will usually choose to live on large ponds as small ponds can quickly run out of food. Ducks can upset a pond's ecosystem. They can eat so many larvae, pond snails and tadpoles that fewer minibeasts survive to have young of their own.

Female mallard and ducklings

Flock of mallards on a pond

Waterbirds can be part of a healthy pond ecosystem, so long as there aren't too many of them.

Brown long-
eared bat

Ponds and visiting animals

In the evening and early in the morning, bats swoop over the surface of ponds in search of a drink. They fly low to scoop up some water.

Bats also hunt for pond insects, snatching mosquitoes, flies, mayflies and dragonflies out of the air. During the day bats return to their roosts in old trees or buildings.

Fox

Other animals drink at the edge
of ponds. Badgers, hedgehogs,
foxes, farm animals and birds
come to ponds for a drink.

Birds also visit ponds to take a bath or hunt
for food. Although kingfishers live and breed
on the banks of rivers and streams, they visit
ponds if there are small fish living there.

Eurasian kingfisher

Many animals
that do not live in
ponds visit them
for a drink or to
hunt for food.

Grass snakes, herons and frogs

A grass snake slides into a pond in search of its favourite prey. It spends most of its life on land, but visits ponds and other freshwater habitats to hunt for frogs, newts and fish.

Grass snake

Grey heron with frog

Grey heron

Another pond visitor is the grey heron. It wades into the water and stands still, waiting for a newt, insect, frog or grass snake to come close. In a flash, it darts forward to grab its prey and swallows it down.

Herons can help control the number of small animals in a pond, but they can upset the balance if they take too many. A heron may visit several different ponds when hunting. When it's time to move on, it flies off, with its long legs stretched out under its body.

Herons and grass snakes are predators at the top of pond food chains. They help to keep pond ecosystems in balance.

29

Ponds in danger

Many ponds have been filled in to make way for roads, homes and buildings, or because farmers no longer use them for their animals.

Over time, other ponds fill up with plants or rubbish and some gradually disappear.

Car tyre in a pond

Ponds near farmland can become polluted when water containing pesticides or fertilisers drains into them.

Sometimes fertilisers make algae grow too strongly and take over a pond, harming everything else in the ecosystem and even killing some animals.

Pond overgrown with algae

This book has explored some of the connections between animals, plants and non-living things in a pond ecosystem. We need to take care of these precious ecosystems so that the connections between these groups are not broken.

Glossary

adapted the way a living thing has changed over time to become better suited to its habitat

algae very simple plants that live in water

amphibian an animal that can live on land and in water

bacteria very tiny living things

ecosystem a community of living things and their environment

fertiliser something added to soil to make plants grow better

food chain the plants and animals linked together by what eats what

gills body parts of some water animals that they use to breathe

habitat the usual home of an animal or plant

hibernate to spend the colder months in a deep sleep

larva the young of fish, insects and some other animals

mate when a male and female animal join together to have young

nymph one stage of the life cycle of some animals before they become adults

photosynthesis the process used by plants to make their own food using carbon dioxide, water, nutrients and energy from sunlight

pesticide a chemical used to kill pests, such as insects

pollinator an animal that moves pollen from flower to flower

pollution damage caused to water, air or wild places by harmful substances, such as chemicals, litter or human waste

predator an animal that hunts and eats other animals

prey an animal that is hunted and eaten by other animals

recycle to break down and reuse materials

roost a place where bats or birds sleep

rot to break down slowly

surface tension the way water droplets form a strong enough surface to be able to hold the weight of very light objects or animals

underground spring a place where water comes naturally to the surface from underground

Books to read

Follow the Food Chain (series)
  by Sarah Ridley (Wayland, 2021)

Predator vs Prey (series)
  by Tim Harris (Franklin Watts, 2020)

The Big Picture: Living Habitats
  by Jon Richards and illustrated by
  Josy Bloggs (Franklin Watts, 2021)

The Great Outdoors: Lakes and Ponds
  by Lisa Regan (Wayland, 2020)

Index